For Joseph and Gabriel,
with all my love
N. D.

For Guy, with love, Uncle Petr

P. H.

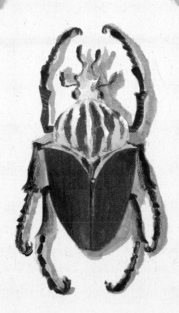

this BOOK
belongs to:

_____

NICOLA DAVIES

—✳✳✳—

SONG of the WILD

A FIRST BOOK of ANIMALS

—✳✳✳—

illustrated by

PETR HORÁČEK

CANDLEWICK PRESS

CONTENTS
—✳✳✳—

BIG AND SMALL
—✳✳✳—

COLORS AND SHAPES
—✳✳✳—

ANIMAL HOMES
—✳✳✳—

ANIMAL BABIES
—✳✳✳—

ANIMALS IN ACTION
—✳✳✳—

BIG and SMALL

Blue Whale

Words can't describe a blue whale's size.

Big and **huge** and **large** don't work.

Even **enormous**, **vast**, **gigantic** aren't enough.

But when you hear a blue whale's blow—

a deep *per-wuffing* sound that makes you think

of caverns, caves, and concert halls—

and see its breath punch upward

like a house-high exclamation mark,

you know that it's the biggest creature

there has ever been.

Song of the Biggest

The ostrich lives in Africa
in grasslands hot and dry,
the biggest bird in all the world—
in fact, too large to fly.

and the Smallest Birds

In Cuba's steamy jungles
where vines curl around the trees
lives the smallest bird—a hummingbird
just bigger than a bee.

This hummingbird could fit inside
an ostrich's big eye.
It seems absurd
that they're both birds,
but here's the reason why:
both have feathers, beaks, and wings,
though they use them for
quite different things.

9

The Bumblebee Bat

Like a flying, furry caramel,
zooming through the secret spaces
in between the treetop leaves,
the bumblebee bat is hunting.

Heart and lungs, brain and blood and bone
are packed inside this tiny body.
The smallest of all mammals
until she has a baby!

Giraffes

The highest eyes in Africa belong to the giraffes.

They see the sunrise first.

Soon the light will slant between the trees

and they'll vanish into dappled shade.

But now the sun is just a sliver only they can see.

Giraffes see the sunrise first!

Elephants

"LOOK!" you say. "Elephants!"

You're right, of course. What else could they be?

But look again. Are they the same?

Is one a little bigger? Does one have smaller ears?

And when they grab food with their trunks,

look closely at the ends:

Are *they* the same? No.

Isn't it nice to know that there

are twice as many kinds

of elephants as you thought:

African and Asian!

Big Lions

Flat out in the shade,

lions lie flopped in a heap, asleep.

But when dusk falls, they'll wake.

Muscles will ripple under their golden coats,

and as they yawn, you'll see their long, sharp teeth.

Little Lions

Teacup small, these little monkeys—
Mama, Papa, and their twins—
go dancing through the treetops.
Golden lion tamarins!

Cute as a Newt

Don't get me wrong: I like frogs,
with their hopping and bopping
and their breaststroke legs.

But there's nothing as cute as a common newt—
their little velvet bodies, smaller than your finger,
and their orange spotted tummies.

No one notices them—they're sort of secret—
but everyone should know
that there's nothing,
no, there's nothing,
that is as cute as a newt.

Komodo Dragon

This dragon has no fire, but its tongue flickers like a flame.

This dragon has no wings, but it can fly through the forest.

Its claws are knives; its bite is poisonous—

whisper its name, Komodo, and beware!

Ants

Ants are always busy:

legs whizzing, feelers touching, tasting.

They leave a scent trail to the food they find

so other ants can find it too.

In no time there's a stream of ants

flowing to the food and back to the nest.

The nest's a maze of tiny tunnels underground.

It holds as many ants as there are people in a city.

Somewhere deep and hidden, the queen is laying eggs

and eggs and eggs that will become more ants.

No wonder ants are always busy

with such a huge family to feed!

Whale Shark

Like a piece of fallen starry sky,

the spotted whale shark cruises by,

swimming the secret depths alone.

As soon as it appears, it's gone.

WHAT AM I ?

Whale sharks aren't whales but great big fish. Bats aren't birds, even though they have wings. How can you figure out which animals belong together?

MAMMAL

Breathes air
Fur
Warm-blooded
Produces milk

BIRD

Breathes air
Beak
Feathers
Warm-blooded
Lays eggs

AMPHIBIAN

Breathes air and water
Smooth, wet skin
Cold-blooded
Lays eggs in water

REPTILE

Breathes air
Dry, scaly skin
Lays eggs (mostly)

SPIDER

Eight legs

CRUSTACEAN

Ten legs

INSECT

Six legs

But what about the blue whale?

Lives in water but breathes air.

No legs but warm-blooded.

Has live babies.

It's a MAMMAL!

FISH

Breathes water
Scales
Fins

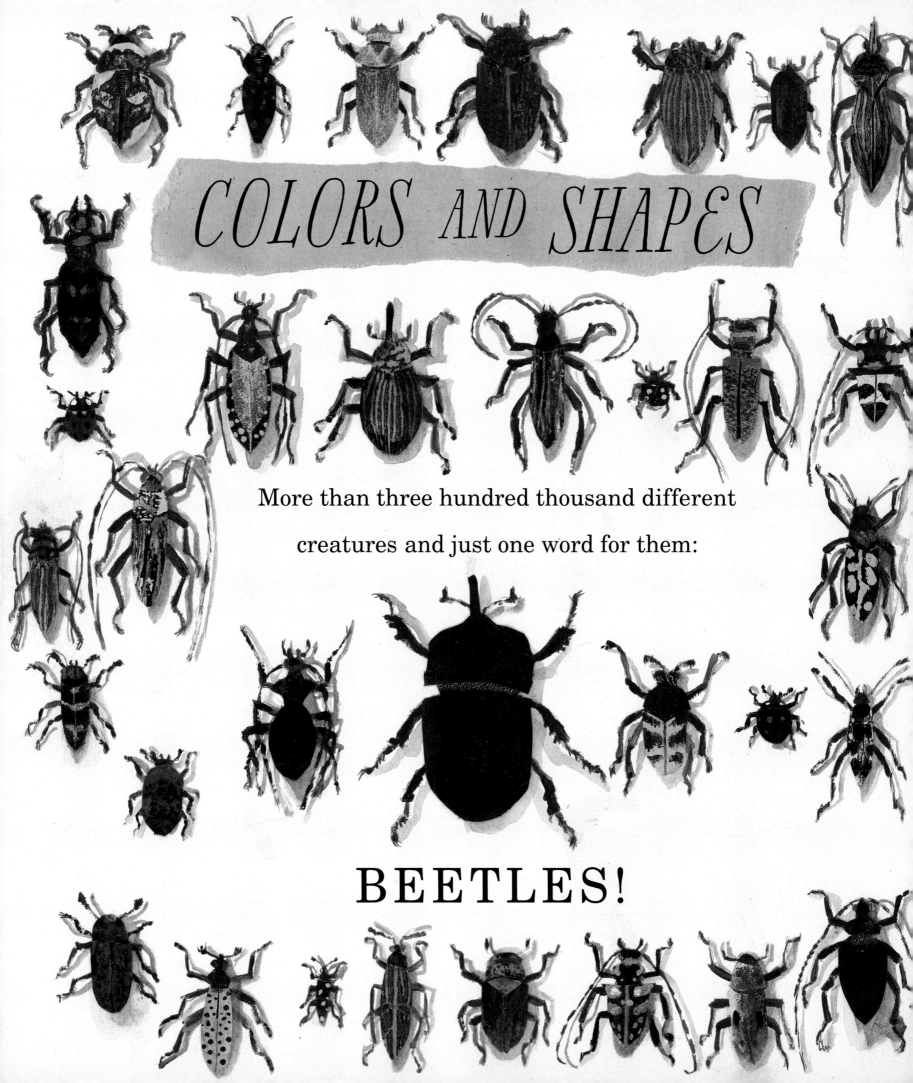

COLORS AND SHAPES

More than three hundred thousand different

creatures and just one word for them:

BEETLES!

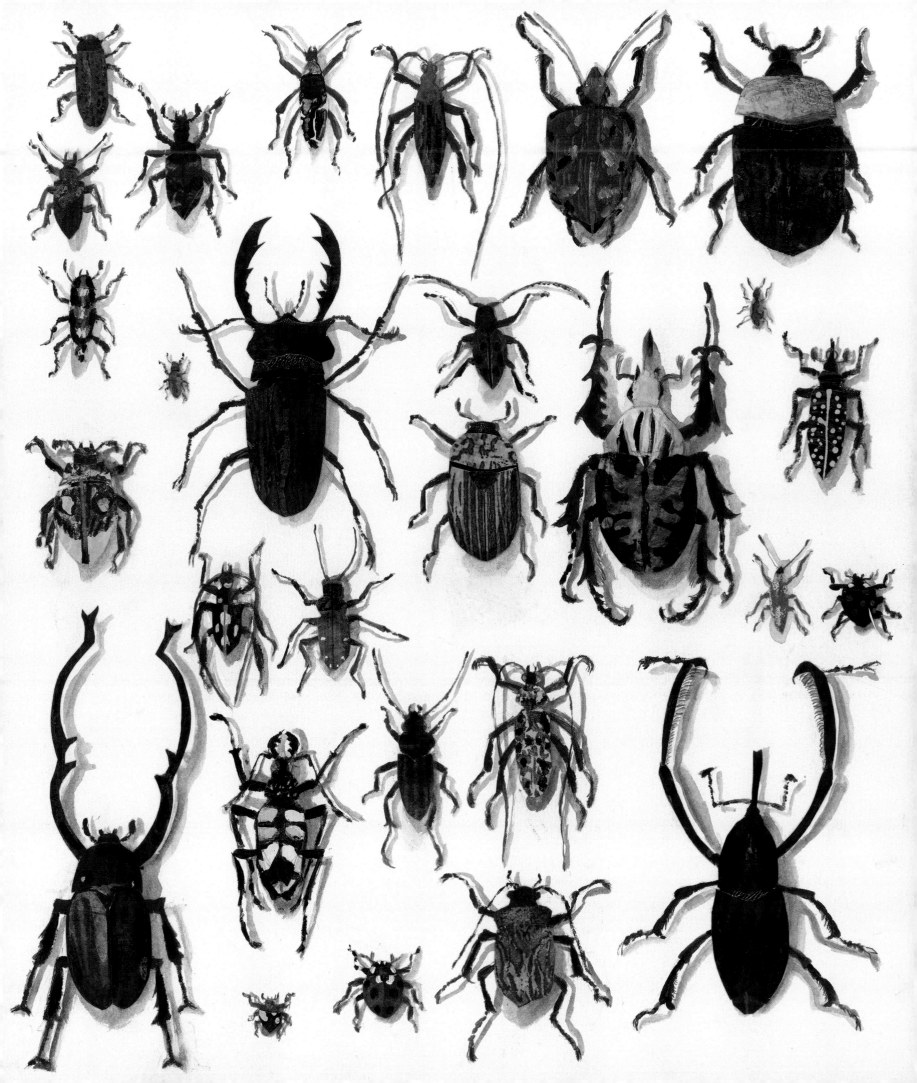

Tiger, Tiger, Orange Striped

Orange tiger in the night,

you'd give all the deer a fright,

but stripes make you disappear from sight;

they won't see you—till you bite!

Flamingos Think Pink

Success for flamingos depends on one thing: being PINK!

They can't find a mate if their feathers are not the brightest PINK

and they don't want to nest if the birds all around them aren't PINK,

so they feed upside down in the mud 'cause their food makes them PINK!

31

Giant Leaf Insect

Somewhere in this tree,
there is a huge insect, as big as your hand.

Somewhere, somewhere
along this branch, hiding, safe from hungry mouths.

Somewhere, somewhere, somewhere,
there's a leaf that's not a leaf but a giant leaf insect.

Somewhere!

Chameleon Song

Chameleons have curly tails
and little toes that grip,
eyes that move on turrets,
long tongues with sticky tips.

They creep around the bushes
and can turn themselves quite green,
till they blend in with the forest
and simply can't be seen.

But if they're feeling lonely,
they can turn from green to blue,
or to any other color,
to say, "I'm fond of you!"

Why Are
Zebras Striped?

Stripes!

Black-white, white-black,

on legs, body, face, back.

Stripes!
White-black, black-white,
vanish in half-light.

Stripes!
White-black, black-white,
flies don't want to bite.

Stripes black, stripes white,
zebra stripes are what we like!

Blue Morpho Butterfly

You don't see much in a rain forest.

It's shadowy and green,

gloomy almost.

All around you, creatures *plink* and *churr*

and whistle, out of sight.

You feel alone.

Suddenly a flash of sapphire,

bigger than a dinner plate:

a butterfly swooping down the path.

It appears and disappears as it flaps its wings,

and leads you on and on . . .

like a dream you can't quite remember.

Camels and Their Humps

Sizzling days, freezing nights:

desert life is tough.

Food? Not much.

Water? Not enough.

Camels have a store of fat, their hump,

that helps them through.

Dromedaries have just one;

Bactrians, two.

Birds of

There are colors dancing in the forest.

Not a jungle party or

visitors from outer space,

but birds of paradise,

shape-shifting with their feathers

to make flashing, popping rainbows

Paradise

that say, "I'm best and brightest!

I'm the one you want!"

Panda Song

High up in the Chinese mountains,
where the bamboo thickets grow,
lives a bear that's most unusual:
black as night and white as snow.

Could it be that its strange color
helps it find another bear
when it tires of being lonesome
and wants to be a pair?

Or is black and white for hiding
in the snow or up a tree,
where the patchy ice or shadows
make it very hard to see?

High up in the Chinese mountains,
the panda walks alone . . .
and the reason for its color
we may never really know.

SPOTS AND STRIPES

Animals use spots and stripes in lots of different ways.
Here are some of them:

The spots on this butterfly
scare off hungry birds.

These spots confuse
bigger fish—they don't
know which end is which!

Spots make leopards hard to see in the shadows.

44

These stripes warn that
this wasp will sting.

Stripes like grassy shadows
help tigers to hide.

These stripes warn that this
snake has a venomous bite.

ANIMAL HOMES

The Beaver Dam

Big trees felled, mud and sticks cleverly piled up.
Who'd imagine that an animal built this?

But now there's a pond, reflecting clouds,
where once a small stream ran,
because the beavers wanted a home
and built a dam.

Weaverbird

First he needs a fresh green ribbon

torn from a blade of elephant grass.

Next a knot tied round a dangling twig,

then a hoop, just big enough to perch in.

Now he makes the roof, walls, and floor.

It's a long job. He needs ribbon after ribbon.

He teases them in and out, one way, then the other.

At last, the entrance:

a downward-pointing tube to keep out snakes.

Then the weaverbird hangs at his front door,

fluttering and singing, waiting and hoping for a mate!

Wolves Howl

Into the big dark silence, the wolves howl.

Their voices reach over the frozen stream,

between the snow-muffled trees,

past the twitching ears of deer and hare,

claiming the land, and all that's in it, as their own.

Snail Shells

A curly suit of armor,

that's the snail's spiral shell.

It protects the snail from drying out,

from hungry mouths as well.

A shell is like a mobile house

and allows a snail to roam.

But if you take one from your garden,

it will find its way back home!

Spiderweb

The spider spans the space between the trees with silk.

Length after length pulled from her body,

smaller than a coffee bean.

Across and down. In, out, and around.

Last, she winds a sticky spiral into the center.

There she sits and waits to feel

the struggling of prey

caught on her silken wheel.

Anemones and Clown Fish

These anemones are not flowers.

They are animals made of stinging fingers

around a hungry mouth.

Without eyes to see or ears to hear,

they touch and sting,

kill and eat.

Only the little clown fish

snuggles in, unstung,

to lay her eggs,

safe in a deadly cradle.

Jellyfish
Go with the Flow

A jellyfish doesn't choose a place to be.

It goes with the flow, where the current takes it.

As long as it can squeeze its see-through body

to push itself along and trawl

its stinging tentacles to catch tiny prey,

it doesn't care, or even notice.

Orangutan
Nest Building

All day, the orangutan meanders

through the treetops with her baby.

She looks as if she's daydreaming,

yet she somehow finds all the best fruit.

Now she's bending branches, halfway up a tree,

dreamily, as if she didn't have a plan.

Yet here's a bed with a twiggy mattress

and a perfect pillow made of leaves.

The evening sky is clear and pink;

there is no sign of rain.

Yet the orangutan has added a canopy to her nest.

Perhaps she knows things that we don't.

White Storks' Nests

People said it was lucky to have a white stork nesting on your house.

They'd put old cartwheels on their roofs, to give the birds a start.

Once, every farm had storks, clattering their beaks up there,

while the humans went about their business down below.

When the marshes were drained, the storks stopped coming.

For years, the cartwheels on the rooftops lay abandoned.

But now there are new wetlands, and the storks are back,

though this time they prefer to nest on pylons!

PARASITES

Dolphins live in the sea, and orangutans live in the jungle. But fleas live on other animals, and there are many other creatures that do so as well. They're called parasites.

Fleas live in other animals' fur. When they're hungry, they bite the animal's skin to suck some of its blood.

Tapeworms live in other animals' guts.
This one likes to live in humans.

Eyelash mites are so
tiny they live in the roots of
your eyelashes. Most adult
humans have them.

Some parasites live in odd places.
This creature lives only on the eyes
of Greenland sharks.

ANIMAL BABIES

First Day Out

Mama polar bear clambers from

her den and sniffs the air.

"Uff! Uff!" she calls,

and her twins appear,

each one smaller than a spaniel.

This is their first day in the world,

and there's a lot to learn:

all about ice and how to stalk a seal.

But for now, rolling down the hill

like a pair of furry snowflakes

will have to do.

Sea Turtle Egg Laying

Eight weeks ago, at night, a mother turtle

crawled up this beach to lay her eggs.

Each one was a soggy Ping-Pong ball

that made a soft, wet *plop*

as it dropped into the hole she'd dug.

She laid a hundred, then she buried them

and threw dry sand in crazy fountains

to cover up the egg-filled hole.

And that was it: her job was done.

She struggled down the beach, back to the sea.

Tonight, the sand she dug danced and wriggled.

Now her babies skeeter toward the ocean.

Baby Gorilla

The newest baby in the forest

opens her chestnut eyes:

she sees there's mist, and green, and trees.

Family, too: sisters, brothers, aunties, cousins,

and her big silver-backed papa.

She snuggles in her mom's strong arms,

her deep, dark fur . . .

and goes back to sleep.

Ways to Get to Water

There are THOUSANDS of kinds of frogs and toads.
Nearly all of them start life as tadpoles. Tadpoles need water to live in,
so most frogs lay their eggs in water. But the ones that *don't*
have found some clever ways of getting to it. . . .

Male midwife toads carry their eggs
around and drop them in a pool when
they're ready to hatch.

Poison arrow frogs carry
their tadpoles on their
backs to rain pools
caught in the leaves
of plants.

Male Darwin's frogs swallow their tadpoles as they hatch so they grow into frogs inside their wet mouths.

Some tree frogs make foamy nests on leaves above a river. The tadpoles hatch and fall into the water.

Dragonfly Babies

In the pond's dark murk
they lurk,
monster babies.

They reach and grab,
grasp and stab,
with catapult jaws.

Again and again
they split their skin,
growing bigger.

Up they climb,
split one last time,
spread grown-up wings:

dragonflies!

Daddy Sea Horse

From a swollen, pregnant pouch,

small fishy sea foals squiggle out.

They've grown from eggs inside the tummy

of their daddy, not their mommy.

Emperor Penguins

Shuffle-shuffle.

That's what emperor daddies do all winter long,

huddled in with a flock of other fathers,

each one shuffling with an egg balanced on his feet,

folded in a flap of skin to keep it warm—

cuddled from the cold.

Shuffle-huddle, shuffle-huddle,

through dark and cruel cold,

through biting blizzards.

They are quiet heroes, waiting

for the *peep peep* of their hatching chick

and the voice of their mate, returning from the sea.

Kangaroo Birth

Blind and pink and naked,

tiny as a jelly bean,

a newborn kangaroo

looks like a worm.

It knows it must climb up

to the safety of its mother's pouch.

She doesn't help much,

and it seems to take forever.

At last, it's there.

Enclosed in warmth and darkness,

it grows into a furry joey.

Soon it'll be hopping out and in again.

The Tender Crocodile

No one thinks of crocodiles as gentle;

tenderness is something for the doves.

But when baby crocodiles are hatching,

it's hard to say they don't get Mother's love.

Their fearsome mom's been waiting for the moment

when the babies start to call her from their nest.

She digs them out and carries one to water,

then comes back and fetches all the rest.

A baby croc is fierce, but still quite tiny;

for many creatures, it's a tasty snack.

Mom sticks around to keep her young protected—

she even lets them ride upon her back.

So when you hear it said that crocs are vicious,

that they're heartless and they'd like to do you harm,

just remember that a croc can be a mommy:

can be tender, can be gentle, can be warm.

EGGS

Many kinds of animals lay eggs, so all sorts of creatures hatch out of them.

Pythons wriggle out of leathery eggs.

Female ocean sunfish lay up to 300 million eggs,
each one just bigger than a comma.

Caterpillars pop out of eggs as small as pinheads.

Ostrich chicks hatch from an egg that's almost as big as a soccer ball.

"Mermaid purses" that you can find on the beach are the egg cases of dogfish and skates.

The Dinner That Got Away

The fastest sprinter on the earth

is racing now for all she's worth.

She bends and stretches like a spring;

like shoes with spikes, her claws dig in.

84

Her tail helps her turn to left and right

to keep her dinner in her sight.

The cheetah's nearly caught her prey—

but in the end, it gets away!

Arctic Tern

White wings, as delicate as paper,
and a body lighter than a cupcake,
but this small bird flies from pole to pole
and back again each year.

If you add up all the journeys
the Arctic tern makes in its life,
they'd reach up to the moon
and back again three times.

Koala Lullaby

High in the gum tree, the koala sleeps,

fluffy as a little cloud, cuddled in the branches.

Sometime, not very soon, it will wake,

eat leaves, and sleep again.

Sleep and sleep and sleep,

while all around, the gum leaves sigh

a never-ending lullaby.

Slow, Slow Sloth

Sloths don't like it on the ground;

they much prefer to hang around

high up in a forest tree,

hooked on by two toes, or by three.

Tiny plants turn their fur green,

so when they're still, they can't be seen.

They munch on leaves, don't do a lot,

but who wants a world where sloths are not?

Fireflies

Green and yellow fairy lights

are twinkling in the summer night.

On-off! On-off! Off-on! Off-on!

They wink and blink and then they're gone.

Each one's a beetle flashing a sign

that says, "Please find me and be mine!"

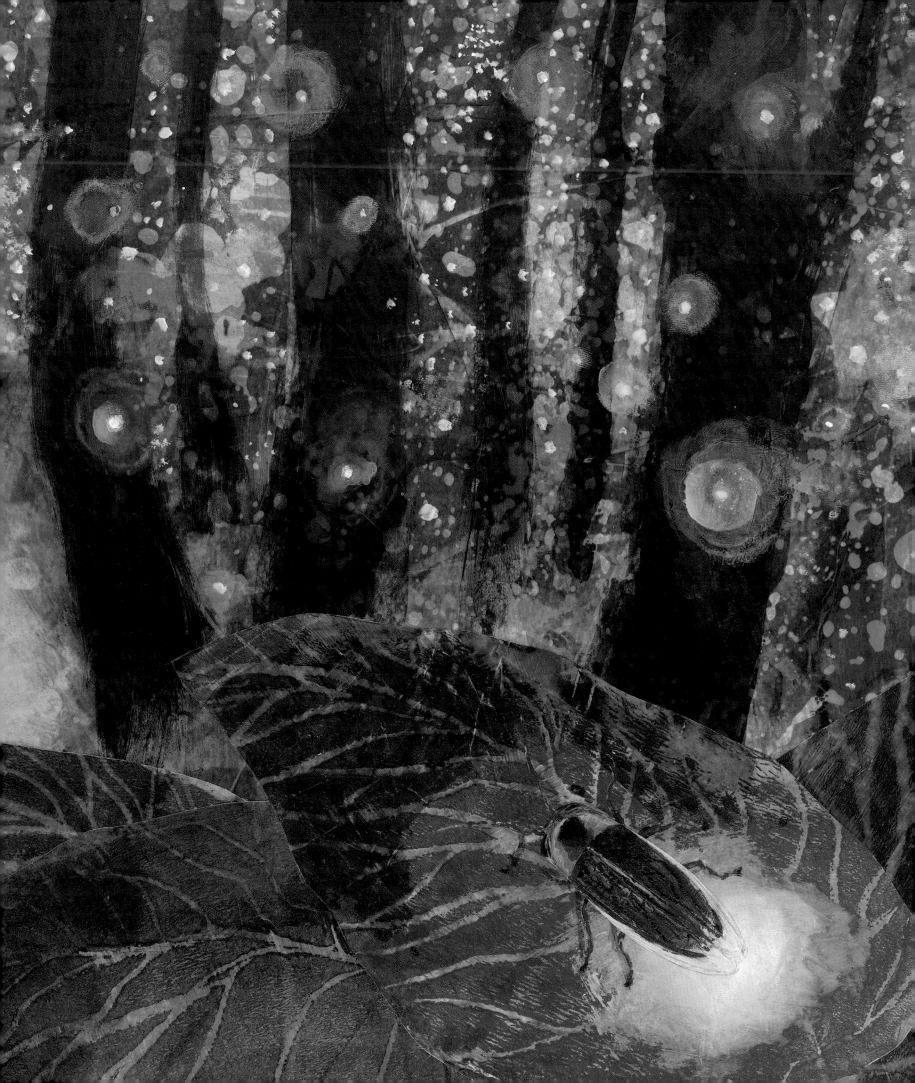

Dancing Bees

Inside the hum and hurry of the hive,

a bee has news to tell her sisters:

Flowers! Flowers! Lots of flowers!

She dances out her message,

a slanting line of steps to give direction

and waggles, counted out to tell how far.

Her sisters fly off in a beeline to the flowers,

collecting nectar, ready for when summer's gone.

Barn Owl

Velvet soft and gleaming white,

the barn owl flies across the night.

Quiet as the floating moon,

it looks, it listens, then swoops down.

The mouse never heard the owl come;

now, just as silently, it's gone.

Monarch Butterflies

There is a grove

where the butterflies come,

in clouds of orange wings.

Like autumn leaves played backward,

they fly up onto the twigs,

clothing, covering, the trees

in a thick coat of living flame

that shimmers as a shiver passes

from wing to wing to wing.

There is a grove

where the butterflies come,

a place of dreams and magic.

The Swiftest Sailfish

Fast and fierce:

fin flouncing, flashing, flexing;

sword swishing, stabbing, slashing.

Small fry flinch and die

as the sailfish feeds, swift and furious.

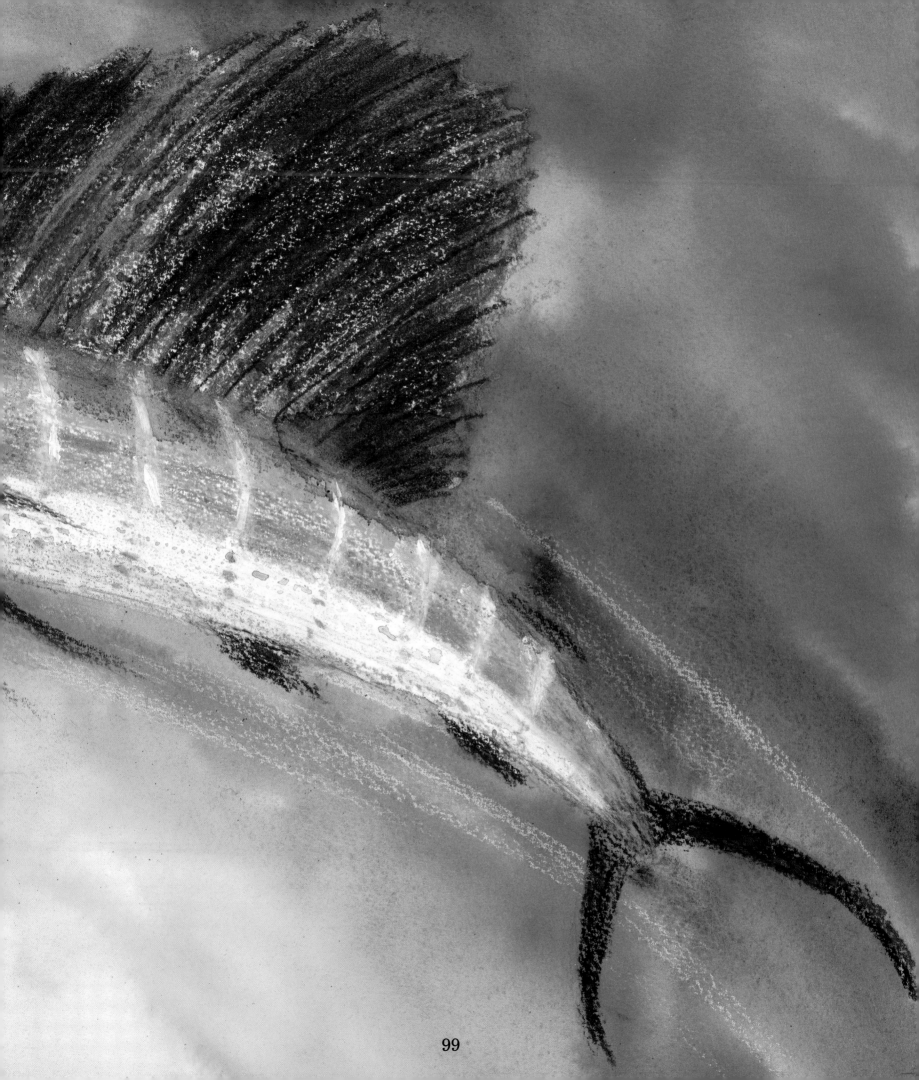

All in the Bite

A viper has no legs to run on,
no claws to grab with,
but it's got a bite.

Its fangs are like hollow needles
injecting poison.
One bite is enough.

It swallows its prey whole,
because a snake can't chew
but only bite.

A viper has no legs to run on,
no claws to grab with,
but it's got a bite.

Corals

A million, trillion, zillion

tiny tentacles and mouths

open-close, open-close,

like miniature umbrellas.

So small! So delicate!

And yet together, over years and years,

they build reefs of stone,

home for rainbow clouds of fish—

and big enough to be seen from space.

The Nightingale and the Humpback Whale

In the middle of the midnight woods

when all is quiet,

the nightingale trills and gurgles,

singing, singing!

Far beneath the silvery ocean,

where the waves can't reach,

the humpback whale booms and burbles,

singing, singing!

They will never hear each other;

only you can tell

their different songs are the same music,

singing, singing!

TOOL-USING ANIMALS

People used to think that only humans used tools.

Now we know that lots of animals do.

Bottlenose dolphins use a bit of sea sponge to protect their noses from cuts when they're searching for food on rocky seabeds.

Chimpanzees use sticks to poke termite mounds and pull out juicy termites.

Capuchin monkeys
use big stones to
crack nuts.

Woodpecker finches on
the Galápagos Islands use
cactus spines like forks to
spear grubs in tree holes.

First U.S. edition 2017

Library of Congress Catalog Card Number 2017956031
ISBN 978-0-7636-9160-8

18 19 20 21 22 CCP 10 9 8 7 6 5 4 3 2

Printed in Shenzhen, Guangdong, China

This book was typeset in New Century Schoolbook and Typnic.
The illustrations were done in mixed media.

Candlewick Press
99 Dover Street
Somerville, Massachusetts 02144

visit us at www.candlewick.com